G000151420

O
Anniversary
of Your Loss

On the Anniversary of Your Loss

written by
Linus Mundy

illustrated by
R.W. Alley

ONE
CARING
PLACE
Abbey Press

Text © 2007 by Linus Mundy
Illustrations © 2007 by Saint Meinrad Archabbey
Published by One Caring Place
Abbey Press
St. Meinrad, Indiana 47577

Library of Congress Catalog Number
2007908208

ISBN 978-0-87029-412-9

Printed in the United States of America

Foreword

No matter how long, no matter how short, a life lived is never lost to those who remember. And the anniversary of a loss is, of course, a very special time to remember...and thereby further the healing. It is a time to take stock of the lessons learned, the hardships endured, the small victories won.

This book offers 38 illustrated bits of wisdom, each offering the reader loving, healing ways to observe and "mark" this anniversary time. The book is meant to guide and console, to inspire and encourage.

The anniversary of a loss is, after all, a time of many mixed emotions, a time of sadness that is mixed, we pray, with opportunity and new hope.

1.

This anniversary is a good time to take stock, to see how far you have come or still need to go. It's a time to review past lessons and plan for what lies ahead. Above all, it's a time to acknowledge that you have made it thus far, despite all the hardship.

2.

How was it that you "made it through" thus far? Think about some of the good choices you have made, the kindnesses you may have received, the healthy ways you have expressed your grief.

3.

It is no crime on this anniversary of loss to be experiencing as sharply as ever all the sadness of your loss. Or there may be a bittersweet tinge, a pang that brings tears that you thought were behind you, perhaps mixed with a hint of better tomorrows.

4.

You may be feeling disappointed that you aren't doing better—since, as others remind you, it's been "a pretty long while now." Don't let anyone accuse you of "wallowing" in grief. Taking time to lean into your sorrow is facing reality.

5.

Don't expect everyone else to remember this anniversary. Even if they do remember, they may be keeping silent as a way to show their care. If you want others to remember, do some gentle reminding and reaching out beforehand.

6.

You may not be feeling much of anything beyond a general sense of loss. Our grief comes in many flavors, and it doesn't follow a calendar.

7.

You may be experiencing what are called "secondary losses" or "secondary griefs." We grieve our lost dreams, the ways our relationships fell short, the things we had or hadn't said or done. Ask God to heal all your hurts.

8.

Turning your grief over to God doesn't mean that the hurting stops. Yet you no longer focus so much on the pain, but rather on the search for spiritual connections with your loved one.

9.

This is a good time to remind people of what you need and want. You wouldn't hesitate to ask for help when it comes to a heavy bag of groceries or a car that is stalled. Why, then, be reluctant to ask for help when your spiritual burden is heavy, or emotional progress is stalled?

10.

Don't hesitate to ask for companionship. Claim those earlier offers about "anything I can do to help." Be specific: Ask someone to drive you to the cemetery or join you for shopping or for lunch. Invite someone to give you a shoulder to cry on.

11.

Sometimes you want to touch or be touched by your loved one who is no longer physically present. You can hold a picture of them close to your heart—or take some favorite clothing of theirs and make a blanket or quilt to wrap around and warm yourself.

12.

Don't hold back the tears if the tears are there. Crying, whether public or private, helps you grieve well and grow stronger.

13.

As you gain a bit of distance from the season of your loss, you may even find yourself crying for joy. Partly, you are grieving your loved one's absence at such happy moments; partly, your loss has given you a new appreciation for the tender, fragile beauty at the core of life.

14.

Continue to honor your loved
one by remembering fondly his
or her best traits—and then
renewing your efforts to emulate
them. How would you yourself
like to be more like him or her?

15.

There are lots of simple ways to remember and commemorate this anniversary and the days surrounding it. Write a one-page story about the life of your loved one. Or get out pictures and clippings and create a memory album for sharing.

16.

Be sure to keep telling the story of your loved one. This is the most genuine way to convey and keep the memory of your loved one alive. Don't forget those special traits or "quirks" that made that someone truly special.

17.

You may find it healing to recall your loved one's wake and funeral, with all its sadness— but also with all the signs of care which surrounded you in those difficult first days. Feel again the warm hugs, the sight of friends gathered to grieve and pray with you.

18.

This anniversary may be the
perfect time for something as
grand as dedicating a public
garden or park in memory of
your loved one—or as simple
as planting a geranium in your
window box.

IN MEMORY OF
SAMUEL ELFKINS

19.

A Native American prayer says to the great Spirit: "Only for a short time have you loaned us to each other." Give thanks to God for having "loaned" this special person to you, and rejoice in knowing that the gift endures.

20.

Present a memorial keepsake to someone—a dish, a pin, a book or memento—that signifies something about your loved one. What a way to honor your loved one's abiding presence.

21.

Be sure to take account of what you have, the people in your life, the kindnesses shown to you, the folks and experiences you still treasure. This will help offset the burden of loss that will always be part of what you carry.

22.

Consider writing a letter to your loved one. This is a way to bare your soul, to say what has been unsaid, and to repeat what has been said but needs to be said again—that love matters and lasts.

23.

Do something that confirms your relationship with your loved one has changed, not ended. That's an anniversary gift to both of you.

24.

Remember the painful things, too, in your relationship with your loved one. All relationships include disappointments and shortcomings. When you express them, you can begin to let them go.

25.

Honor life itself—and the Giver of life. Thank God for the gifts of life and time you have shared. God tells us something astonishing about time and life and love: They go on and on—beyond the first anniversary, the tenth anniversary, beyond the hundredth.

26.

The word "celebrate" isn't only about joy; it's about observing, paying attention, and noticing. So go ahead and celebrate the life of a loved one who has meant—and continues to mean—so much to you.

27.

Honor this period as a rite of
passage, giving yourself the
right to pass to a new stage
in your grieving and healing.
Healing means coming to more
and more acceptance of your
loss, while at the same time
moving forward with your
own life.

28.

Consider a public—or private—worship service. Many faith traditions celebrate a worship service in memory of a particular person, pausing in prayer to remember with you the special blessing your loved one was and still is to you.

29.

Something as important, challenging, and profound as grieving requires solitude at times. You need to be fully present, to pay attention, to hear your inner voice, in order to move through this great and significant work.

30.

Don't be afraid to have a good time. A life lived without good times is not much of a life. Times of sorrow come, but they also go, we pray. And when the time is right, let yourself be moved to new experiences and new joys.

31.

As grief subsides, you
sometimes wish to cling to it
out of a fear that if your grief
disappears, your memory of your
loved one will disappear, too.
Fear not. Memory is stronger
than grief.

32.

While you are celebrating this rite of passage, you will be getting a gift as well as giving one. It will be the gift of a loving, lasting communion that binds you to your loved one for eternity.

33.

Think back on your long period of sorrow. Recall the gifts that you have uncovered and discovered during this difficult time. What have you learned about yourself and your inner resources?

34.

The turns of the calendar mark the passing of time. But time works its healing magic only when it is used well. Use your time in facing the truth of your sorrow—as well as the abiding truth that love has no end.

35.

Look ahead; plan just one thing for the future. Think big, if you can: a change of job, a special vacation, redecorating the house. Or think small: lunch with a friend, making that phone call you've been delaying.

36.

As you look ahead, ask yourself which of your relationships need attention, to whom you need to express your affection while there is still time. Mark your calendar to extend a friendly invitation.

37.

The best anniversary gift you can give to yourself and your departed loved one is the gift of healing—even if it's just the beginning.

38.

It's time now to wish for a
"happy new year." Time to hope
and pray for new tomorrows
filled with purpose and
happiness. May they open up
for you. And may love be what
you remember most and what
you carry with you.

Linus Mundy is Director of Publications at Abbey Press. He is the founder of One Caring Place and its "CareNotes" line of publications which have comforted many who are grieving, ill, or distressed.

Illustrator for the Abbey Press Elf-help Books, **R.W. Alley**, also illustrates and writes children's books, including *Making a Boring Day Better—A Kid's Guide to Battling the Blahs*, a recent Elf-help Book for Kids. See a wide variety of his works at: www.rwalley.com

The Story of the Abbey Press Elves

The engaging figures that populate the Abbey Press "elf-help" line of publications and products first appeared in 1987 on the pages of a small self-help book called *Be-good-to-yourself Therapy*. Shaped by the publishing staff's vision and defined in R.W. Alley's inventive illustrations, they lived out the author's gentle, self-nurturing advice with charm, poignancy, and humor.

Reader response was so enthusiastic that more Elf-help Books were soon under way, a still-growing series that has inspired a line of related gift products.

The especially endearing character featured in the early books—sporting a cap with a mood-changing candle in its peak—has since been joined by a spirited female elf with flowers in her hair.

These two exuberant, sensitive, resourceful, kindhearted, lovable sprites, along with their lively elfin community, reveal what's truly important as they offer messages of joy and wonder, playfulness and co-creation, wholeness and serenity, the miracle of life and the mystery of God's love.

With wisdom and whimsy, these little creatures with long noses demonstrate the elf-help way to a rich and fulfilling life.

Elf-help Books

...adding "a little character" and a lot
of help to self-help reading!

Friendship Therapy	#20174
Christmas Therapy (color edition) $5.95	#20175
Happy Birthday Therapy	#20181
Forgiveness Therapy	#20184
Keep-life-simple Therapy	#20185
Acceptance Therapy	#20190
Keeping-up-your-spirits Therapy	#20195
Slow-down Therapy	#20203
One-day-at-a-time Therapy	#20204
Prayer Therapy	#20206
Be-good-to-your-marriage Therapy	#20205
Be-good-to-yourself Therapy	#20255

Book price is $4.95 unless otherwise noted.
Available at your favorite gift shop or bookstore—
or directly from One Caring Place, Abbey Press
Publications, St. Meinrad, IN 47577.
Or call 1-800-325-2511.
www.carenotes.com